turpiculo puella naso
insapiens
caenum
nasum rhinocerotis
peronatus arator
SULTATOR
vastus animus
cincinnatus
schoenobates
larva
molestae
odiosus mihis
verbero
LONGINQUUS PISCIS
senex hircosus
livide
ex hara producte
DELICIAS
SALIVA MUCUSQUE
ursis asperior pilosiorque
sordidique lichenes
febriculosi scorti
CAENUM
MALA PITUITA NASI
sceleratus
senex nequissime
RIDICULI
ULCUS ACRE
stulte
LIPPUS
lacticulosus
CAEPA CIRRATA
lanifuga
verbex
LIGNEA
SATELLITES
ILLEPIDAS

11 12 13 14 15 16 17 18 19 20

First Published in 1998 by Ebury Press, an imprint of Ebury Publishing

Penguin
Random House
UK

Concept, design and translations © Michelle Lovric 1998

Michelle Lovric and Nikiforos Doxiadis Mardas have asserted their rights to be identified as the authors of this Work in accordance with the Copyright, Designs and Patents Act 1988

Ebury Press is part of the Penguin Random House Group of Companies whose addresses can be found at
global.penguinrandomhouse.com

A CIP catalogue record for this book is available from the British Library

Conceived and compiled by Michelle Lovric
Research and modern translations by Nikiforos Doxiadis Mardas and Michelle Lovric
Cover designed by Michelle Lovric and Lisa Pentreath
Internals designed by Michelle Lovric and AB3

Manufactured in China by Imago

The registered trademarks, logos and trade names in this book have been reproduced with the kind permission of the companies concerned. They are strictly copyright, and must not be reproduced without the company's express permission.

About the editors...
Michelle Lovric has created over thirty illustrated anthologies, including several about love. Her book, *Love Letters AN ANTHOLOGY OF PASSION* was a *New York Times* bestseller. She has also published three novels. She has collaborated with Nikiforos Doxiadis Mardas to create a series of new translations of Greek and Latin Poetry: *The Sweetness of Honey and the Sting of Bees – Words of Love from the Ancient Mediterranean* (Aurum Press, £9.99)

Nikiforos Doxiadis Mardas lives in London and Athens. He graduated from the University of Cambridge with a first class degree in Classics, and he has been immersed in the physical and academic worlds of the Ancient Mediterranean throughout his life.

The editors gratefully acknowledge permission to reproduce illustrations from *Heck's Pictorial Archive of Art & Architecture*, edited by J. G. Heck, published by Dover publications, Inc. Copyright © 1994 Dover Publications, Inc.

The editors would also like to thank Ann Alwis, Nicola Carr, Rick Litchfield, and Sophie Monro-Davies for their help researching and compiling this book.

This book is dedicated to Andreas Laskaris and Trevor Sather – verbal assassins still practising ancient arts.

ISBN 9780091864453

HOW TO
INSULT
ABUSE &
INSINUATE IN
CLASSICAL LATIN

SALEM AC LEPOREM

Naughty but nice

Catullus, poem 26

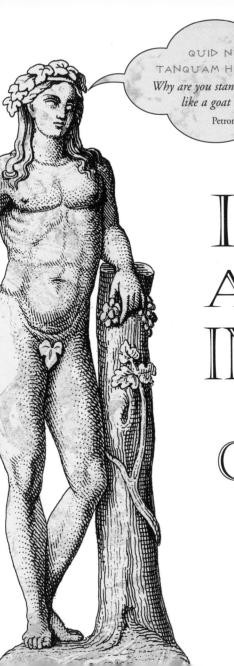

QUID NUNC STUPES
TANQUAM HIRCUS IN ERVILIA?

*Why are you standing there staring at me
like a goat in a field of vetch?*

Petronius, Satyricon

HOW TO
INSULT
ABUSE &
INSINUATE
IN
CLASSICAL
LATIN

MICHELLE LOVRIC &
NIKIFOROS DOXIADIS MARDAS

EBURY PRESS
LONDON

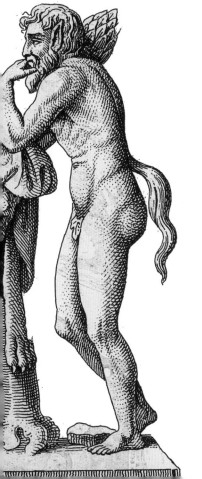

TU PRAETER
OMNES UNE DE
CAPILLATIS

Of all the long-haired twits,
you are the shaggiest.
Catullus, poem 37

CONTENTS

PRAEFATIO·

Introduction

PECCAVIMUS

We confess

We have quoted every Latin author here entirely out of context. We have on occasion taken translators' liberties with the nominative case, adding vocative exclamations where they have no business to be. We have gouged out gerundives and annihilated innocent ablative absolutes. We have inserted intermittent innuendos, and provided passing past participles. We have also ousted the odd obscenity, or at least confined it to the ellipsis of history. However, we have tried, with great earnestness and sincerity, to convey the spirit of what the ancient writers were expressing, wrapped in the real imagery that they used. We have also tried to recreate some of the diabolical delight these ancient writers took in the rich resource of their language. Latin luxuriates in alliteration, puns and double entendres — and so, here, have we.

IMPROBISSIMUM VERO LIBELLUM SCRIPSIMUS

We have written a very wicked book indeed

But with the best possible motives. There are times when a terse Anglo-Saxon monosyllable simply cannot express the full horror of the miseries of human life, as inflicted upon us by other miserable specimens of humanity. We want you to be able to relieve your tensions with an explosive expletive, and to devastate those who do you wrong with an ancient, but still potent missile newly excavated from classical literature. Express your outrage in the words of the Great. ***Make enemies and impress people.***

Michelle Lovric & Nikiforos Doxiadis Mardas,
Covent Garden, January 1998.
HORTI TEMPLORUM, IANUARIO, MXMXCVIII

DE INSIGNIBUS SCRIPTORIBUS...

Apuleius (fl. c. AD155)
Latin writer, born in Madaurus in Africa. His wonderful *Metamorphoses* is the story of one Lucius who, after keeping the wrong company, manages to get himself transformed into an ass. Also known as 'The Golden Ass' it is the only novel in Latin that has survived in its entirety.

Aulus Gellius (c. 130—c. 180)
Roman writer, educated in Athens. His *Attic Nights* is comprised of short sections on a wide variety of topics, including one on the use of insults. The work was compiled during the winter nights in Attica for the entertainment and education of his children.

Catullus (Gaius Valerius Catullus) (c. 84—54BC)
Roman poet. His magnificent insults are aimed mainly at personal enemies who fail to meet the poet's exacting standards of urbanity and elegance. In the following century, Martial, another virtuoso of invective, hailed him as his master.

Cicero (Marcus Tullius) (106—43BC)
Roman orator, statesman and philosopher. His extremely active political life made him many enemies, and his surviving speeches preserve for us something of the wit, vigour and tireless energy of the insults with which he assailed them. His damning orations against Verres and Catiline are a rich source of invective.

Horace (Quintus Horatius Flaccus) (65—8BC)
Roman poet. Admired for his mastery of form and elegance of language, his famous celebrations of the good things in life sometimes give way to the harshest of invective. Unsavoury old women were a favourite target.

Juvenal (Decimus Iunius Iuvenalis) (fl. early 2nd century)
Roman satirist. In the first of his sixteen satires, he declares that he has no choice but to write satire when faced with the daily corruption of Rome. His tone is bitterly ironic and his invective venomous.

Martial (Marcus Valerius Martialis) (c. 40—103)
Roman poet. Born in Bilbilis in Spain, he spent most of his life in Rome, where between the years 86 and 98 he produced his first 11 books of epigrams. In them, insult is elevated to art form, and his victims face an elegant whirlwind of abuse of a violence not unleashed since the time of Catullus, 150 years before.

Ovid (Publius Ovidius Naso) (43BC—c. AD18)
Roman poet. Subtly ironic and faultlessly elegant as a commentator on love, in his *Ibis*, Ovid displays a violence of language and feeling to match the most unbridled invective of any age.

LONGINQUUS PISCIS
Far-out fish-face!
Ovid, Ibis

CRUDE VULTUR
Dyspeptic vulture!
Ovid, Ibis

NUGATOR
Humbug!
Plautus, Miles Gloriosus

PERMITIES
Leech!
Plautus, Miles Gloriosus

ABOUT THE EMINENT AUTHORS...

Persius (Aulus Persius Flaccus) (34—62)

Roman satirist. Born in a wealthy Etrurian family, he studied in Rome under the Stoic philosopher Cornutus. He died young, leaving six satires expounding his stoic morality; he is said to have been an unassuming and kind man and accordingly his invective lacks the raw malice of some more bad-tempered contemporaries.

Petronius (Titus Petronius Arbiter) (d. AD65)

Roman writer. His novel the *Satyricon* is a send-up of decadent life in the Roman empire of the 1st century. The most famous section of the book concerns a wildly extravagant and depraved dinner party given by the vulgar millionaire Trimalchio.

Plautus (Titus Maccius Plautus) (c. 250—184BC)

Roman comic playwright. Twenty of his plays, lively and straightforward adaptations from Greek New Comedy of the 4th and 3rd centuries, are among the rare survivors from this early period of Latin literature. Stock characters and situations — the clever slave, the braggart soldier and the topsy-turvy love affair — provide a healthy range of insults.

Priapea

A body of poems in honour of Priapus, the enormously-endowed god of fertility, guardian deity, and professional scarecrow. There are eighty of the poems in all, collected in the first century, and of these we know that the third in the collection is by Ovid. Otherwise authorship is uncertain, their common bond being magnificent — and unfortunately mostly unprintable — obscenity.

Sallust (Gaius Sallustius Crispus) (86—35BC)

Roman historian. He gave up politics — having served as governor of the province of Numidia in 46 — for history writing, and his choice of colourful protagonists for his historical monographs, as well as his deep-seated hostility towards the nobility, earns him a place among the mud-slingers of his age.

Suetonius (Gaius Suetonius Tranquillus) (b. c. 70)

Roman biographer. His position as secretary at the imperial palace, a position he lost in 122 for an alleged indiscretion involving the Emperor Hadrian's wife, afforded him access to the imperial archives on which he drew for his *Lives of the Caesars*. These are rich in anecdote, colour and gossip, if not always in historical impartiality.

Virgil (Publius Vergilius Maro) (70—19BC)

Roman poet. He is chiefly celebrated for the epic poem the *Aeneid*, the Latin answer to Homer's *Iliad* and *Odyssey*. Virgil's style is usually graceful and somewhat stately. Most of the insults that can be attributed to Virgil come from the mouths of his various heroines, reproaching the hero Aeneas, for perfidious desertion.

NEQUISSIMUM ET PERIURUM CAPUT
Utter dregs and dross of a man!
Apuleius, Metamorphoses IX

SALIVA MUCUSQUE
Spit and slime!
Catullus, poem 23

PRAEDO AMENTISSIME
Outrageously rabid robber!
Cicero, In Pisonem

ME VITUPERAS? FUR! ETIAM FUR! TRIFURCIFER!
Are you abusing me? Thief! Thief of Thieves! Thief, thief thief!
Plautus, Aulularia

WITLESS

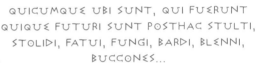

RES PERTRICOSA EST, COTILE,
BELLUS HOMO.
A pretty fellow is a waste of space, Cotilus.
Martial, Epigrams III.63

MUFRIUS, NON MAGISTER.
You're not a guru, you're a gorilla.
Petronius , Satyricon

QUICUMQUE UBI SUNT, QUI FUERUNT
QUIQUE FUTURI SUNT POSTHAC STULTI,
STOLIDI, FATUI, FUNGI, BARDI, BLENNI,
BUCCONES...
*Of all the past, present and future fatheads, idiots,
imbeciles, mushrooms, morons, hare-brains and
chipmunk-cheeks...!*
Plautus, Mnesilochus

AH, LASSITUDINEM HERCLE VERBA TUA
MIHI ADDUNT, ENICAS.
*Everything you say is so unbearably boring, by
Hercules, that it's murder by monotony.*
Plautus, Mercator

CERTO SCIO, OCCISAM SAEPE SAPERE PLUS
MULTO SUEM.
*I'm quite sure that a stuck pig is regularly more
discerning than you.*
Plautus, Miles Gloriosus

VASTUS ANIMUS.
His mind is one vast wasteland.
Sallust, Bellum Catilinae

INSIPIENS

TAM AUTEM ERAS EXCORS, UT TOTA IN ORATIONE TUA
TECUM IPSE PUGNARES, NON MODO NON COHAERENTIA
INTER SE DICERES, SED MAXIME DISIUNCTA ATQUE
CONTRARIA, UT NON TANTA MECUM QUANTA
TIBI TECUM ESSET CONTENTIO.

*You were such a moron that throughout your speech you were
at war with yourself, firing out statements which were not
just inconsistent, but which were utterly devoid of any
coherence or logic, to the point where your adversary
in battle stopped being me and became yourself.*
Cicero, Philippicae II

URBANUS TIBI,
CAECILI, VIDERIS.
NON ES, CREDE MIHI.
QUID ERGO? VERNA ES.

*You fancy yourself a colosseum of wit, Caecilius.
I don't think so. What do I think?
You're a pigsty.*
Martial, Epigrams I.41

SENEX NEQUISSIME
Silly old sod!
Plautus, Mercator

• 13 •

DULCIA CUM
TANTUM SCRIBAS
EPIGRAMMATA SEMPER ET CERUSSATA
CANDIDIORA CUTE,
NULLAQUE MICA SALIS NEC AMARI FELLIS IN ILLIS
GUTTA SIT, O DEMENS, VIS TAMEN ILLA LEGI

Whenever you write epigrams they come out sickly sweet,
purer white than the icing on a wedding cake.
Not a pinch of salt, not a bit of bitter bite,
but you, in your insanity, want people to read them.
Martial, Epigrams VII.25

MIRARIS VETERES,
VACERRA, SOLOS
NEC LAUDAS NISI MORTUOS POETAS.
IGNOSCAS PETIMUS, VACERRA: TANTI
NON EST, UT PLACEAM TIBI, PERIRE

You go on and on about only the ancients, Vacerra,
and you don't approve of a poet unless he's dead.
Well, you'll have to excuse me, Vacerra,
but death is too high a price to pay
for your praise.
Martial, Epigrams VIII.69

CUR NON MITTO MEOS TIBI,
PONTILIANE, LIBELLOS?
NE MIHI TU MITTAS, PONTILIANE, TUOS.
You ask why I haven't sent you any of my poetry, Pontilianus?
I'm afraid you might send me some of yours in return.
Martial, Epigrams VII.3

VERSUS SCRIBERE POSSE TE DISERTOS
AFFIRMAS, LABERI: QUID ERGO NON VIS?
You insist that you can craft elegant poetry, Laberus.
Why won't you then?
Martial, Epigrams VI.14

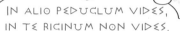

> **IN ALIO PEDUCLUM VIDES,**
> **IN TE RICINUM NON VIDES.**
>
> *You can see the lice on others, but not the*
> *bugs on yourself.*
>
> Petronius, Satyricon

NUNC SUNT CRURA PILIS ET SUNT TIBI
PECTORA SAETIS HORRIDA, SED MENS EST,
PANNYCHE, VULSA TIBI.

As it is, your legs are bristling with hair, and your chest is a deep-
shag rug, but your mind, Pannychus, has been plucked smooth.

Martial, Epigrams II.36

AD MANDATA CLAUDUS
CAECUS MUTUS MANCUS DEBILIS.

When it comes to following orders you're a lame, blind, mute,
maimed wreck of a man.

Plautus, Mercator

HOMO ET HUMANITATIS EXPERS ET VITAE
COMMUNIS IGNARUS.

A man completely destitute of all human kindness, and utterly
ignorant of all social observance.

Cicero, Philippicae II

SI DECEM HABEAS LINGUAS, MUTUM ESSE
ADDECET.

Even if you had ten tongues, you ought to hold them all.

Plautus, Mnesilochus

NIL BENE CUM FACIAS,
FACIAS TAMEN OMNIA BELLE,
VIS DICAM QUID SIS? MAGNUS ES ARDALIO.

You do nothing well. But everything you do, you do in style.
How should we describe you? You are just a great big piece of fluff.
Martial, Epigrams II.7

ES VILIOR ET LEVIOR.
You are cheaper and crummier (than I thought you were).
Catullus, poem 72

CUI NEQUE SERVUS EST NEQUE ARCA NEC
CIMEX NEQUE ARANEUS
You don't have a servant, or piggy-bank,
or even a bed-bug or a spider.
Catullus, poem 23

ODIOSUS MIHIS.
You're just a bad smell, as far as I'm concerned.
Plautus, Mnesilochus

NATES PILOSAS,
FILI, NON POTES ASSE VENDITARE.
Sonny-boy, you couldn't sell your hairy rump
for a penny.
Catullus, poem 33

NON EGO TUAM
EMPSIM VITAM VITIOSA NUCE.
Your life's not worth a rotten nut to me.
Plautus, Miles Gloriosus

WORTHLESS

VILISSIMUS

STERTIS ADHUC? LAXUMQUE CAPUT CONPAGE
SOLUTA OSCITAT HESTERNUM DISSUTIS UNDIQUE MALIS?
EST ALIQUID QUO TENDIS, ET IN QUOD DERIGIS ARCUM?

Are you still snoring? Is your slack head almost snapped on its stalk, with your face unzipped
by the yawns earned in yesterday's debaucheries? Do you have any goals in life? Is there
any point to your life?

Persius, Satire III

NEMO CONGRESSU, NEMO ADITU, NEMO SUFFRAGIO,
NEMO CIVITATE, NEMO LUCE DIGNUM PUTET

No one thinks you're worth his attention, his time, a vote, a place in society,
or even the light of day.

Cicero, In Vatinium

INDILIGENS CUM PIGRA FAMILIA...

You're a good-for-nothing slacker with a dysfunctional family...

Plautus, Miles Gloriosus

OBLATRATRIX
Yapping cow!
Plautus, Miles Gloriosus

...DISCINCTAQUE IN OTIA NATUS

...Born to lounge around in naked sloth.

Ovid, Amores I.9

LINGUA FACTIOSI, INERTES OPERA.

All talk and no action.

Plautus, Mnesilochus

GORMLESS

LONGOS IMITARIS.
You pretend you are one of the big boys.
Horace, Satires II.3

CURRIS, STUPES, SATAGIS, TANQUAM MUS IN MATELLA.
All you do is run back and forth with a stupid expression, jittery as a rat in roasting pot.
Petronius, Satyricon

HAERES NEQUIQUAM CAENO CUPIENS EVELLERE PLANTAM.
Struggling in vain to lift yourself out of the mud, you
just get sucked deeper in.
Horace, Satires II.7

TU URBANUS VERO SCURRA, DELICIAE POPLI.
You really are the village idiot, the play-thing of the people.
Plautus, Miles Gloriosus

QUIS UMQUAM ADPARITOR TAM HUMILIS,
TAM ABIECTUS?
What cringing sycophant ever sank so low,
so ignominiously?
Cicero, Philippicae II

SIBILUM METUIS?
Are you afraid of hisses?
Cicero, In Pisonem

NE ACCLAMETUR
TIMES?
Are you afraid to be booed?
Cicero, In Pisonem

INFELIX
No-hoper!
Cicero, In Pisonem

POETA
Poet!
Cicero, In Pisonem

CHARMLESS

NON AMO TE, SABIDI, NEC POSSUM DICERE QUARE:
HOC TANTUM POSSUM DICERE, NON AMO TE.

I don't like you, Sabidus, and I can't say why.
But I can say this much for sure: I don't like you.

Martial, Epigrams I.32

Note — this couplet was the inspiration for
Tom Brown's famous epigram:

I do not love thee, Doctor Fell.
The reason why I cannot tell;
But this alone I know full well,
I do not love thee, Doctor Fell.

TE NEMO TUORUM
VIDERE VULT, OMNES
ADITUM, SERMONEM,
CONGRESSUM TUUM FUGIUNT

None of your loved ones wants to lay eyes
on you; everyone beats a hasty
retreat from your approach, your
conversation, and your company.

Cicero, Pro Sestio

QUID MIHI REDDAT AGER QUAERIS, LINE, NOMENTANUS?
HOC MIHI REDDIT AGER: TE, LINE, NON VIDEO.

You want to know what I get out of my little plot
at Nomentum, Linus?
This is what I get out of my little plot, Linus:
I don't have to see you there.

Martial, Epigrams II.38

• 22 •

ODI TE QUIA BELLUS ES, SABELLE.
RES EST PUTIDA BELLUS; ET SABELLUS.
BELLUM DENIQUE MALO QUAM SABELLUM.
TABESCAS UTINAM, SABELLE, BELLE!

I hate you because you're a pretty-boy, Sabellus.
In my book, prettiness is a dirty word. And so is Sabellus.
I prefer war to Sabellus.
Sabellus, go to hell!
(Prettily.)

Martial, Epigrams XII.39

SINE VENVSTATE

QUANDO FABAE NOBIS MODIUM FARRISVE DEDISTI,
CUM TUA NILIACUS RURA COLONUS ARET?
QUANDO BREVIS GELIDAE MISSA EST TOGA TEMPORE BRUMAE?
ARGENTI VENIT QUANDO SELIBRA MIHI?
NIL ALIUD VIDEO QUO TE CREDAMUS AMICUM
QUAM QUOD ME CORAM PERDERE, CRISPE, SOLES.

You may have your Nile-side acres tended by a local farmer,
*but when have you given **me** a single bean or a handful of wheat?*
When have I ever received even the thinnest of togas to help me through the icy winter days?
When did I see even a half-pound of silver from your hands? In fact, as far as I can see, the only
single thing which makes me think of you as a friend, Crispus, is your habit of
farting in my presence.

Martial, Epigrams X.15

GENUS, AUCTE,
LUCRI DIVITES HABENT IRAM:
ODISSE QUAM DONARE VILIUS CONSTAT.

The rich, Auctus, see their irritability as just another industry:
hating is more cost-effective than giving.

Martial, Epigrams XII.13

SCORPIONEM PRAE MORUM
ACRITUDINE VULGUS APPELLAT.

The people call him the Scorpion,
on account of his poisonous personality.

Apuleius, Metamorphoses IX

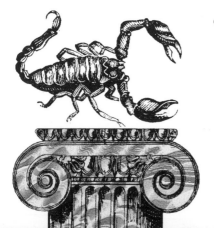

GRATUITO POTIUS MALUS ATQUE CRUDELIS ERAT.

He was gratuitously nasty, mean and cruel, whenever possible.

Sallust, Bellum Catilinae

INPLICATA INSCIENTIA INPUDENTIA EST

His ignorance and his insolence are inextricably intermingled.

Cicero, Philippicae II

ILLE SONAT QUO
MORDETUR GALLINA MARITO.

He makes a noise like a rooster nagging his hen.

Juvenal, Satire 3

LEGLESS

ACCUBANTES IN CONVIVIIS, COMPLEXI MULIERES IMPUDICAS, VINO LANGUIDI, CONFERTI CIBO, SERTIS REDIMITI, UNGUENTIS OBLITI, DEBILITATI STUPRIS ERUCTANT SERMONIBUS SUIS CAEDEM BONORUM ATQUE URBIS INCENDIA.

Reclining at their banquets, groping their whores, drooping with drink, stuffed full of food, draped with garlands, weighed down with oily scents, worn out by their debauchery, they belch out their plans for the slaughter of honest men and the burning of the city.

Cicero, In Catilinam II

DEDITI VENTRI ATQUE SOMNO.

Men dedicated to the belly and to lying in bed.

Sallust, Bellum Catilinae

VINO, GANEIS, LENOCINIIS, ADULTERIISQUE CONFECTUM.

Worn out with drink, debauchery, pimping and adultery.

Cicero, Pro Sestio

NEMO POTEST DICERE UTRUM ISTE PLUS BIBERIT AN VOMUERIT AN EFFUDERIT.

No one can say whether he spent more time drinking, or vomiting, or relieving himself.

Cicero, In Pisonem

FOEDA CONVIVIA.

What a disgusting dinner-party!

Ovid
Ibis

EBRIOSUS

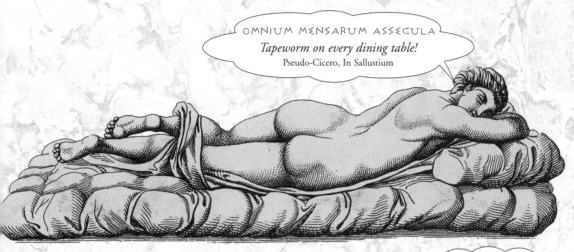

TAMQUAM ALTA IN DOLIA LONGUS
DECIDERIT SERPENS, BIBIT ET VOMIT.
She drinks and vomits like a sinewy snake that has falllen
into a deep vat of wine.
Juvenal, Satire 6

HESTERNO FETERE MERO QUI CREDIT ACERRAM,
FALLITUR: IN LUCEM SEMPER ACERRA BIBIT.
Anyone who thinks that Acerra stinks of yesterday's wine
*Is quite mistaken: Acerra always keeps drinking until **tomorrow**.*
Martial, Epigrams I.28

SEXLESS

> INACHIAM TER NOCTE POTES, MIHI SEMPER AD UNUM MOLLIS OPUS.
>
> *You can manage Inachia three times a night, but with me you're never even up for the first round.*
>
> Horace, Epode 12

> QUAERIS CUR NOLIM TE DUCERE, GALLA? DISERTA ES. SAEPE SOLOECISMUM MENTULA NOSTRA FACIT.
>
> *You're wondering why I don't want to lead you down the aisle, Galla? You're an intellectual, but my organ commits the occasional solecism.*
>
> Martial, Epigrams XI.19

> UMBRA ES AMANTIS MAGIS QUAM AMATOR.
>
> *You're not a real lover, you're just the shadow of a real lover.*
>
> Plautus, Miles Gloriosus

> DEFORMIS ANUSQUE.
>
> *A twisted old hag.*
>
> Martial Epigrams VII.75

> QUO FUGIT VENUS, HEU, QUOVE COLOR?
>
> *Where has all your sex-appeal gone? Ah, how did your blossom wither?*
>
> Horace, Odes IV.13

> FIS ANUS ET TAMEN VIS FORMOSA VIDERI LUDISQUE ET BIBIS IMPUDENS ET CANTU TREMULO POTA CUPIDINEM LENTUM SOLLICITAS.
>
> *You're well past it, but still you want to look like a model and run with the fun crowd, and drink like a fish, and, even though you're maudlin with booze, you try to get a rise out of unwilling Cupid with a quavering song.*
>
> Horace, Odes IV.13

QUO VENUS ABHORRET

MALE ME
MAREM PUTATIS?
So you think this stud's been knackered?
Catullus, poem 16

MOLLIOR CUNICULI CAPILLO,
VEL ANSERIS MEDULLULA
VEL IMULA ORICILLA VEL PENE
LANGUIDO SENIS SITUQUE ARANEOSO.
*You are softer than rabbit's fur,
or goose's down, or a dainty little ear-tip,
or the decrepit organ of an old geezer,
not to mention the cobwebs that
hang there.*
Catullus, poem 25

SED INCITAT ME PECTUS
ET MAMMAE PUTRES, EQUINA
QUALES UBERA, VENTERQUE MOLLIS ET FEMUR
TUMENTIBUS EXILE SURIS ADDITUM.
*But of course what really gets me going about you is those dirty dugs
hanging off your chest, like the nipples of an old nag, your spongy
belly, and those wasted thighs atop your
bulbous legs.*
Horace, Epode 8

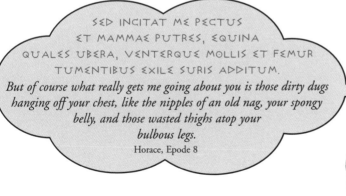

MAIALIS
Gelded grunter!
Cicero, In Pisonem

GRACELESS

CHAR: QUA FORMA ESSE AIEBANT IGITUR?
EUT: EGO DICAM TIBI: CANUM, VARUM, VENTRIOSUM,
BUCCULENTUM, BREVICULUM, SUBNIGRIS OCULIS, OBLONGIS MALIS,
PANSAM ALIQUANTULUM.
CHAR: NON HOMINEM MIHI, SEB THENSAURUM NESCIO QUEM
MEMORAS MALI.

Char: So how did they say that man looked?
Eut: I'll tell you: he was a pint-sized little man with grey hair, knock-knees, a big fat
belly, a gaping mouth, black bags under his eyes, lantern-jawed, with splayed feet.
Char: He's not a man, he's a compendium of weirdness.
Plautus, Mercator

MEDIISQUE IN NARIBUS INGENS
GIBBUS ET ACRE MALUM SEMPER STILLANTIS OCELLI.

He had a huge carbuncle in the middle of his mug,
And an acrid ooze of nastiness always dribbling from his eye.
Juvenal, Satire 6

HUNC VERO ACUTO CAPITE ET
AURIBUS LONGIS,
QUAE SIC MOVENTUR UT
SOLENT ASELLORUM

His head is a pointy cone and he flaps his
elongated ears just like a donkey.
Martial, Epigrams VI.39

COLOR EI EXANGUIS, FOEDI
OCULI, CITUS MODO MODO
TARDUS INCESSUS; PRORSUS IN FACIE
VOLTUQUE VECORDIA INERAT.

His skin was bloodless, his eyeballs festering, he
was now scampering, now dragging his feet; in
short, his rabid state was clearly written on his
features and his bearing.
Sallust, Bellum Catilinae

INLEGANS

DE CATHEDRA QUOTIENS SURGIS — IAM SAEPE
NOTAVI — PEDICANT MISERAE, LESBIA, TE TUNICAE.
QUAS CUM CONATA ES DEXTRA, CONATA SINISTRA
VELLERE, CUM LACRIMIS EXIMIS ET GEMITU:
SIC CONSTRINGUNTUR GEMINA SYMPLEGADE CULI,
UT NIMIAS INTRANT CYANEASQUE NATIS.

Whenever you get up from your chair
— I've spotted this several times already —
your unfortunate robe sodomises you, Lesbia.
You try your hand at yanking it out,
first with the right, then with the left,
but withdrawal can only be won with tears and screams.
The twin peaks of your posterior exert this vice-like grip
on whatever enters the superabundance of your granite buttocks.
Martial, Epigrams XI.99

O AUDACIAM IMMANEM
What monstrous audacity!
Cicero
Philippicae II

HORRIDIOR GLANDEM RUCTANTE MARITO.
She is even shaggier than her acorn-belching husband.
Juvenal, Satire 6

NEQUE ILLI
IAM MANET UMIDA CRETA COLORQUE
STERCORE FUCATUS CROCODILI.
Even the damp powder and the cosmetic
colour, distilled from dried crocodile
dung, won't stick to her any more.
Horace, Epode 12

PITHECIUM HAEC
EST PRAE ILLA ET
SPINTURNICIUM.
*Oh, but compared to **her**, this one's*
nothing but a baby baboon or the
ill-omened offspring of the
penultimate dodo-bird.
Plautus, Miles Gloriosus

CUR SPLENIATO SAEPE PRODEAM MENTO
ALBAVE PICTUS SANA LABRA CERUSSA,
PHILINE. QUAERIS? BASIARE TE NOLO.

*Are you wondering why I go about these days with my chin
shrouded in bandages and my perfect lips smeared with
thick white ointment?
I don't want to have to kiss you.*
Martial, Epigrams X.22

UVIS ARIDIOR PUELLA PASSIS ...
QUAE SUCO CARET UT
PUTRISQUE PUMEX.

*This girl, less succulent than a
shrivelled grape ... is as juicy as a
crumbling pumice stone.*
Priapea 32

SALVE, NEC MINIMO PUELLA NASO
NEC BELLO PEDE NEC NIGRIS OCELLIS
NEC LONGIS DIGITIS NEC ORE SICCO
NEC SANE NIMIS ELEGANTE LINGUA

*Greetings, lady,
Not under-endowed in the nose department,
with not so very beautiful a foot,
nor exactly deep black eyes,
also lacking long slim fingers,
and with a mouth I couldn't really call dry —
with none too pretty a tongue inside it....*
Catullus, poem 43

TU LICET ET MANIBUS
BLANDIS ET VOCIBUS INSTES
TE CONTRA FACIES IMPERIOSA
TUA EST.

*You can make as many sorties as you
like with your seductive hands and
your flattering words, but your face
will always remain your own worst
enemy.*
Martial, Epigrams VI.23

RUBOREM
FERREO CANIS
EXPRIMAMUS ORE
*Let's squeeze a blush out of
that bitch's metallic mug.*
Catullus, poem 42

MENTIRIS FICTOS UNGUENTO, PHOEBE, CAPILLOS
ET TEGITUR PICTIS SORDIDA CALVA COMIS.
TONSOREM CAPITI NON EST ADHIBERE NECESSE:
RADERE TE MELIUS SPONGEA, PHOEBE, POTEST.

You've used dye to forge a false head of hair, Phoebus,
concealing your contemptible cranium with painted-on curls;
so there's really no need to call in the barber,
a wet sponge will have you clean-shaven in no time.

Martial, Epigrams VI.57

TURPICULO PUELLA NASO
Little potato-noselette!
Catullus, poem 41

FIANT ABSENTES ET TIBI, GALLA, COMAE,
NEC DENTES ALITER QUAM SERICA NOCTE REPONAS,
ET IACEAS CENTUM CONDITA PYXIDIBUS,
NEC TECUM FACIES TUA DORMIAT...

Galla, your hair's original owner was someone else's head,
And at night you put aside your teeth,
Just like you put aside your silks.
You lie, dismantled, in a hundred little boxes:
Your face does not sleep with you.

Martial, Epigrams IX.37

TU PUELLA NON ES
You're no spring chicken.
Martial, Epigrams II.41

NE TIBI HERCLE HAUD
LONGEST OS AB INFORTUNIO.
By Hercules, misfortune and your face
are never far apart.
Plautus, Mnesilochus

FACIES TUA CONPUTAT
ANNOS.
Your years are notched up on
your face.
Juvenal, Satire 6

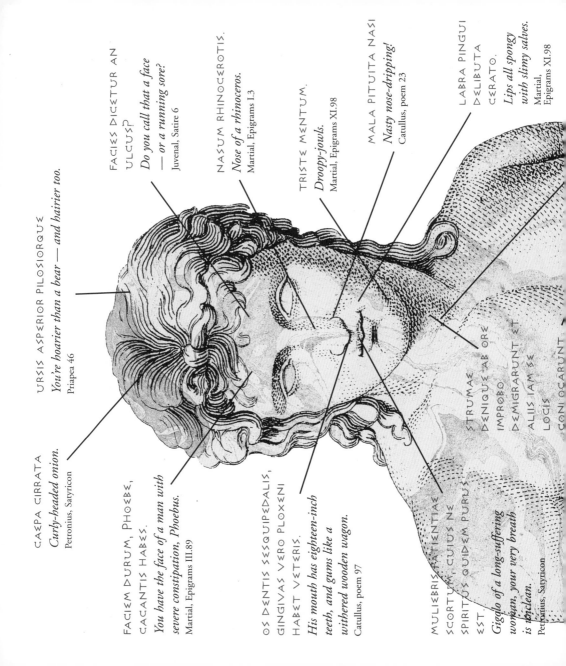

FACIES DICETUR AN
ULCUS?
*Do you call that a face
— or a running sore?*
Juvenal, Satire 6

URSIS ASPERIOR PILOSIORQUE
You're hoarier than a bear — and hairier too.
Priapea 46

NASUM RHINOCEROTIS.
Nose of a rhinoceros.
Martial, Epigrams I.3

TRISTE MENTUM.
Droopy-jowls.
Martial, Epigrams XI.98

MALA PITUITA NASI
Nasty nose-dripping!
Catullus, poem 23

LABRA PINGUI
DELIBUTA
CERATO.
*Lips all spongy
with slimy salves.*
Martial,
Epigrams XI.98

CAEPA CIRRATA
Curly-headed onion.
Petronius, Satyricon

FACIEM DURUM, PHOEBE,
CACANTIS HABES.
*You have the face of a man with
severe constipation, Phoebus.*
Martial, Epigrams III.89

OS DENTIS SESQUIPEDALIS,
GINGIVAS VERO PLOXENI
HABET VETERIS.
*His mouth has eighteen-inch
teeth, and gums like a
withered wooden wagon.*
Catullus, poem 97

STRUMAE
DENIQUE AB ORE
IMPROBO
DEMIGRARUNT ET
ALIIS IAM SE
LOCIS
CONLOCARUNT

MULIEBRIS PATIENTIAE
SCORTUM, CUIUS NE
SPIRITUS QUIDEM PURUS
EST.
*Gigolo of a long-suffering
woman, your very breath
is dirty-clean.*
Petronius, Satyricon

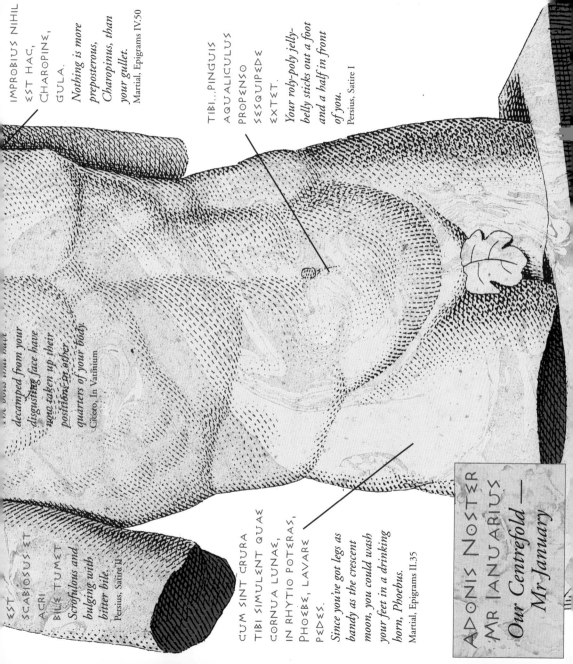

IMPROBIUS NIHIL EST HAC, CHAROPINE, GULA.

Nothing is more preposterous, Charopinus, than your gullet.
Martial, Epigrams IV.50

TIBI..PINGUIS AQUALICULUS PROPENSO SESQUIPEDE EXTET.

Your roly-poly jelly-belly sticks out a foot and a half in front of you.
Persius, Satire I

EST SCABIOSUS ET ACRI BILE TUMET

...decamped from your disgusting face have taken up their position in other quarters of your body.
Cicero, In Vatinium

Scrofulous and bulging with bitter bile.
Persius, Satire II

CUM SINT CRURA TIBI SIMULENT QUAE CORNUA LUNAE, IN RHYTIO POTERAS, PHOEBE, LAVARE PEDES.

Since you've got legs as bandy as the crescent moon, you could wash your feet in a drinking horn, Phoebus.
Martial, Epigrams II.35

ADONIS NOSTER
MR IANUARIUS
*Our Centrefold —
Mr January*

MALO△

FOETOREM EXTREMAE LATRINAE.

You are the stench of a low-life latrine.

Apuleius, Metamorphoses I

GERMANA INLUVIES, RUSTICUS, HIRCUS, HARA SUIS

FU! OBOLUISTI ALIUNUS,

Pooey! You stink of garlic! Home-grown dung, bumpkin, billy-goat, pig-pen!

Plautus, Miles Gloriosus

SORDIDIQUE LICHENES.

Rancid ringworm.

Martial, Epigrams XI.98

EX HARA PRODUCTE

Ex-tenant of a pigsty.

Cicero, In Pisonem

UNGUENTUM FUERAT, QUOD ONYX MODO PARVA GEREBAT:
OLFECIT POSTQUAM PAPYLUS, ECCE, GARUM EST.

A moment ago there was perfume in the little alabaster j...

FOO MT

Then Papylus stuck his nose in it. Now look — it's fish-juice. Martial, Epigrams VII.94

AURICULAM MARIO GRAVITER MIRARIS OLERE. AURICULUM.

TU FACIS HOC: GARRIS, NESTOR, IN

You seem surprised that Marius' ear smells so disgusting, Nestor.

It's your fault: You are always chattering in his ear. Martial, Epigrams III.28

QUI SUDOR VIETIS ET QUAM MALUS UNDIQUE MEMBRIS

CRESCIT ODOR.

What a sweat and what a stink suffuses her senile sinews! Horace, Epode XII

CAENUM LUTULENTE PUSULAEVE LUCENTES Pile of pus. Martial, Epigrams XI.98

Dirt-bag! Cicero, In Pisonem

Filth! Cicero, In Pisonem

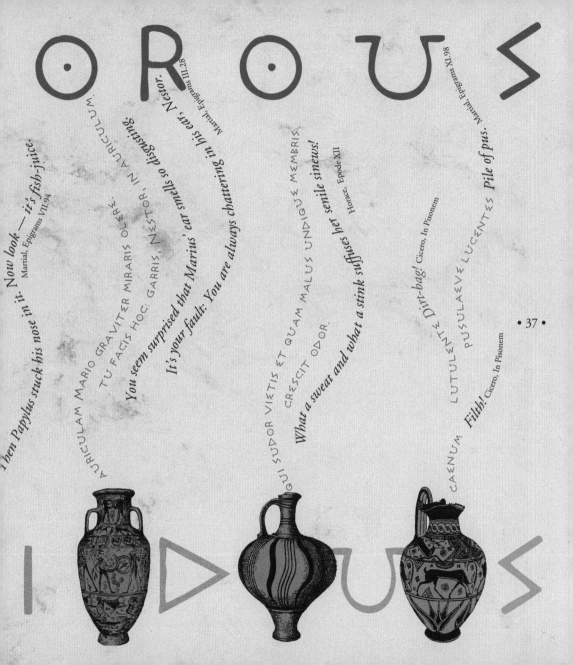

TIBI FERTUR
VALLE SUB ALARUM TRUX HABITARE CAPER.
HUNC METUUNT OMNES.
NEQUE MIRUM: NAM
MALA VALDEST
BESTIA, NEC QUICUM BELLA PUELLA CUBET.

The word is that a rank goat inhabits your armpits.
That's what's sending them running. It's no surprise:
for it's a real hairy monster you've got there
and not at all the type of thing
a beautiful girl wants to lie down with.

Catullus, poem 49

ZOILE, QUOD SOLIUM
SUBLUTO PODICE PERDIS,
SPURCIUS UT FIAT, ZOILE, MERGE CAPUT.

Zoilus, you ruin the bath by rinsing your rear end in it,
but if you really want to insult it, Zoilus,
stick your head in it.

Martial, Epigrams II.42

NAM QUOTIENS FUTUIT,
TOTIENS ULCISCITUR AMBOS:
ILLAM AFFLIGIT ODORE, IPSA PERIT PODAGRA
Every time he makes love, it's a massacre.
He savages her with his stink,
he himself is ravaged by his gout.
Catullus, poem 71

QUOD SICCA REDOLET PALUS LACUNA,
...PISCINAE VETUS AURA QUOD MARINAE,
QUOD PRESSA PIGER HIRCUS IN CAPELLA,
LASSI VARDAICUS QUOD EVOCATI,
...MAESTORUM QUOD ANHELITUS REORUM,
QUOD SPURCAE MORIENS LUCERNA LEDAE,
...QUOD VULPIS FUGA, VIPERAE CUBILE,
MALLEM QUAM QUOD OLES OLERE, BASSA.
The stink emanating from the brackish swamp,
...or the antediluvian stench of a salt-water pond,
or a musty old goat panting over his nanny,
or the old boot of a dog-tired ex-soldier,
...or the halitosis of miserable defendants in the dock,
or the sputtering oil-lamp of perverted Leda,
...or a fox in flight, or a viper's lair,
I'd rather smell of any of these, Bassa,
than smell of you.
Martial, Epigrams IV.4

NON (ITA ME DI AMENT)
QUICQUAM REFERRE PUTAVI,
UTRUMNE OS AN CULUM OLFACEREM AEMILIO.
NILO MUNDIUS HOC, NILOQUE IMMUNDIOR ILLE,
VERUM ETIAM CULUS MUNDIOR ET MELIOR:
NAM SINE DENTIBUS EST.
God help me, I didn't think there was much in it:
whether I sniffed Aemilius' mouth or his rear end.
The former is no fresher, the latter is no fouller.
..But, come to think of it, his ***rear end*** *is far fresher and finer:*
because at least it's got no teeth.
Catullus, poem 97

MISOGYNIST

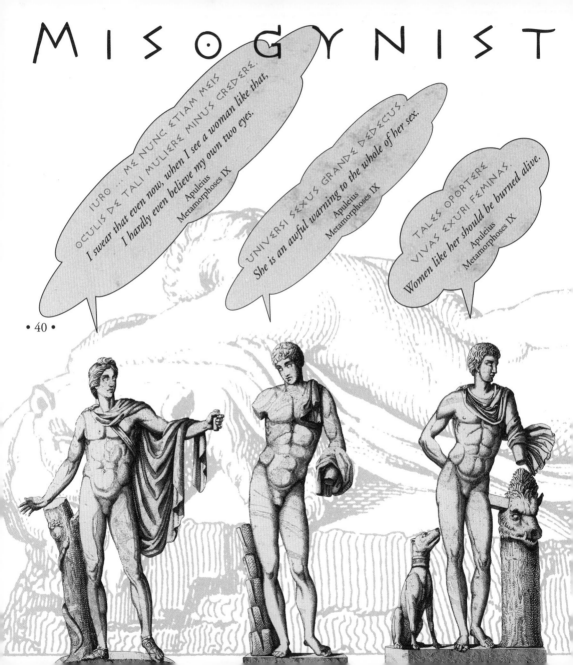

IURO ... ME NUNC ETIAM MEIS
OCULIS DE TALI MULIERE MINUS CREDERE.
I swear that even now, when I see a woman like that,
I hardly even believe my own two eyes.
Apuleius
Metamorphoses IX

UNIVERSI SEXUS GRANDE DEDECUS.
She is an awful warning to the whole of her sex.
Apuleius
Metamorphoses IX

TALES OPORTET
VIVAS EXURI FEMINAS.
Women like her should be burned alive.
Apuleius
Metamorphoses IX

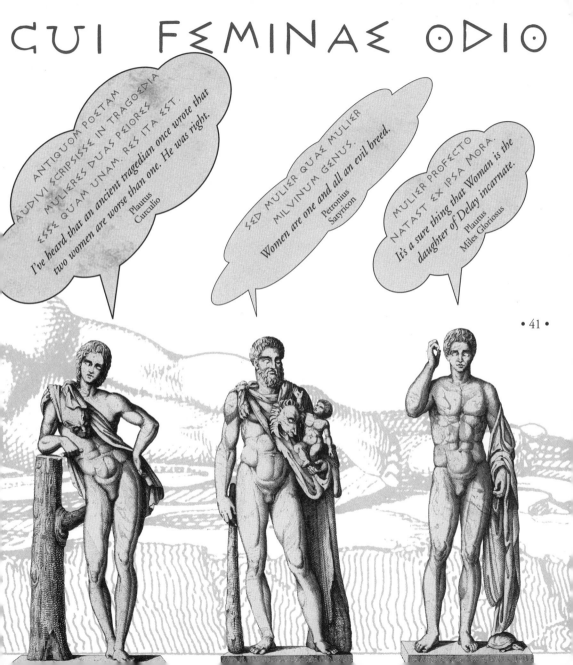

CUI FEMINAE ODIO

ANTIQUOM POETAM
AUDIVI SCRIPSISSE IN TRAGOEDIA
MULIERES DUAS PEIORES
ESSE QUAM UNAM. RES ITA EST.
*I've heard that an ancient tragedian once wrote that
two women are worse than one. He was right.*
Plautus
Curculio

SED MULIER QUAE MULIER
MILVINUM GENUS.
Women are one and all an evil breed.
Petronius
Satyricon

MULIER PROFECTO
NATAST EX IPSA MORA.
*It's a sure thing that Woman is the
daughter of Delay incarnate.*
Plautus
Miles Gloriosus

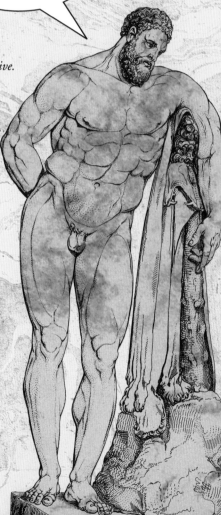

BONA UXOR SUAVE DUCTUST,
SI SIT USQUAM GENTIUM
UBI EA POSSIT INVENIRI

To take a good woman as your wife is a marvellous thing — or at least it would be if there was anywhere on earth you could find one.

Plautus, Miles Gloriosus

DESPERANDA TIBI SALVA CONCORDIA SOCRU.

Give up all hope of peace as long as your mother-in-law is alive.

Juvenal, Satire 6

SED MULIER CUPIDO QUOD DICIT AMANTI
IN VENTO ET RAPIDA SCRIBERE OPORTET AQUA.

*What a woman says to her amorous lover —
you might as well write it on the wind
and running water!*

Catullus, poem 70

VERBA PUELLARUM,
FOLIIS LEVIORA CADUCIS,
INRITA, QUA VISUM EST, VENTUS
ET UNDA FERUNT.

*Any word that comes out of a woman's mouth
is bound to be as lightweight as a falling leaf —
a waste of breath, to be wafted away
at the whim of the wind and the waves.*

Ovid, Amores II.16

NON EGO POSSUM QUAE
IPSA SESE VENDITAT TUTARIER.

*How am I supposed to keep an eye on a woman who is
always on the market?*

Plautus, Miles Gloriosus

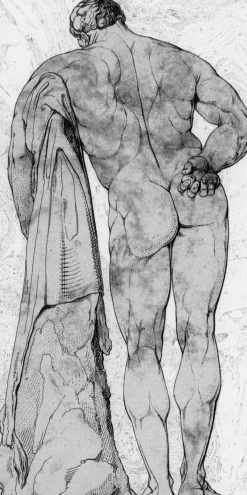

MALA
MULIER MERS EST.

Women are soiled goods.
Plautus
Miles Gloriosus

NAM MULIER HOLITORI
NUMQUAM SUPPLICAT, SI QUAST MALA:
DOMI HABET HORTUM ET
CONDIMENTA AD OMNIS MORES MALEFICOS.

*A truly evil woman doesn't need to beg at the apothecary's
door for her supplies: in her own back yard she cultivates
sauces to complement every sort of sin.*
Plautus, Miles Gloriosus

UBERIBUS SEMPER
LACRIMIS SEMPERQUE PARATIS
IN STATIONE SUA ATQUE
EXPECTANTIBUS ILLAM.

*Tears? She always has plenty in stock, and always
at the ready, standing on guard awaiting her
instructions regarding the manner
of their despatch.*
Juvenal, Satire 6

OMNIA PRORSUS UT IN QUANDAM
CAENOSAM LATRINAM IN EIUS ANIMUM
FLAGITIA CONFLUXERANT.

*Her soul was like some quaggy latrine into which
every imaginable iniquity had flowed.*
Apuleius, Metamorphoses IX

MOECHA TURPIS.

Shameful slut !
Catullus, poem 52

INVISA

Abominable female!
Virgil, Aeneid II

MOLESTAE

Insufferable women!
Plautus, Miles Gloriosus

DISREPUTABLE
IMPROBISSIMUS

PESSIME
Worst of the worst!
Horace, Satires II.7

MALUS.
An all-round bad-guy.
Catullus, poem 5

INFANDUM
Unspeakable!
Virgil, Aeneid I

SCELERATUS
Ruffian!
Cicero, In Pisonem

SCHOENOBATES
Low-life trapeze-artist!
Juvenal, Satire 3

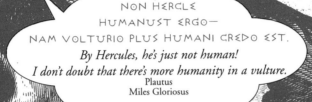

NON HERCLE
HUMANUST ERGO—
NAM VOLTURIO PLUS HUMANI CREDO EST.
By Hercules, he's just not human!
I don't doubt that there's more humanity in a vulture.
Plautus
Miles Gloriosus

DESINET ESSE PRIUS CONTRARIUS IGNIBUS UMOR,
IUNCTAQUE CUM LUNA LUMINA SOLIS ERUNT;
PARSQUE EADEM CAELI ZEPHYROS EMITTET ET EUROS...
ET VER AUTUMNO, BRUMAE MISCEBITUR AESTAS,
ATQUE EADEM REGIO VESPER ET ORTUS ERIT:
QUAM MIHI SIT TECUM POSITIS, QUAE SUMPSIMUS, ARMIS
GRATIA, COMMISSIS, IMPROBE, RUPTA TUIS.
PAX ERIT HAEC NOBIS, DONEC MIHI VITA MANEBIT,
CUM PECORE INFIRMO QUAE SOLET ESSE LUPIS.

Fire and water will forget their age-old enmity.
The sun's rays will stick fast to the moon,
The same gust of wind will blow eastwards and westwards,
Spring will consort with autumn, and winter with summer,
And the sun will rise and set at the very same spot.
All of this must take place, before you and I
Lay down the weapons we have ranged against each other,
*And only **then**, you bastard, will we bring back from the dead the friendship*
Which your grotesque crimes have smashed to smithereens.
Until I breathe my final breath, the only peace we will declare
Will be the kind that exists
Between the wolves and the defenceless sheep.
Ovid, Ibis

SUBLESTA FIDE.
Your fidelity is featherweight.
Plautus, Mnesilochus

FRETIS ACRIOR HADRIAE
CURVANTIS CALABROS SINUS.
More tempestuous than the wild waves of Hadria twisting round the curving coastline of Calabria.
Horace, Odes I.33

PETULANS, PROTERVO, IRACUNDO ANIMO, INDOMITO, INCOGITATO,
SINE MODO ET MODESTIA SUM, SINE BONO IURE ATQUE HONORE,
INCREDIBILIS INPOSQUE ANIMI, INAMABILIS, INLEPIDUS VIVO,
MALEVOLENTE INGENIO NATUS.
Impossible, impudent, bad-tempered, wilful, thoughtless,
Immoderate and immodest, no good at all and up to no good,
Cynical and out of control, unlovable, thoroughly ill-mannered,
Born bad.
Plautus, Mnesilochus

VISCERIBUS MISERORUM ET SANGUINE VESCITUR ATRO.
He feeds on the flesh and dark blood of unfortunates.
Virgil, Aeneid III

IMMANISSIMUM AC FOEDISSIMUM MONSTRUM
Gross and putrid monster.
Cicero, In Pisonem

INTOLERABILIS

O TENEBRAE, LUTUM, SORDES, O PATERNI GENERIS OBLITE,
MATERNI VIX MEMOR

O heart of darkness, of dirt, of degradation, forgetful of your father's fathers,
with scarcely a memory of your mother's mothers!

Cicero, In Pisonem

NULLANE RES POTUIT CRUDELIS FLECTERE MENTIS
CONSILIUM? TIBI NULLA FUIT CLEMENTIA PRAESTO,
IMMITE UT NOSTRI VELLET MISERESCERE PECTUS?

Could nothing sway the decision of your cruel mind?
Was there no humanity in you to move your heartless heart
in compassion for me?

Catullus, poem 64

QUOD MARE CONCEPTUM SPUMANTIBUS EXPUIT UNDIS.

What sea retched you, its creature, up out of its foamy waves?

Catullus, poem 54

QUAENAM TE GENUIT SOLA SUB RUPE LEAENA?

What lioness spawned you under what godforsaken crag?

Catullus, poem 64

HAEC TE, SI ULLAM PARTEM HABES SENSUS,
LACERAT, HAEC CRUENTAT ORATIO.

If there is even a smidgen of human warmth in you, my words
will rend your heart in bloody torture.

Cicero, Philippicae II

O PRAELIGATUM PECTUS!

Your heart is just a hardened artery.

Plautus, Mnesilochus

MEDIOCRITER

Is there any lust which has never shone in your eyes, any crime which your hands ha

Cic

CUI DUBIUM
POTEST ESSE,
QUIN
OPULENTIAM
ISTAM EX
SANGUINE ET
MISERIIS CIVIUM
PARARIS?

*Who could doubt
that you have reaped
this opulent wealth of
yours from the blood
and misery
of the people?*
Pseudo-Sallust
In Ciceronem

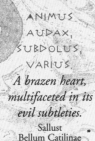

ANIMUS
AUDAX,
SUBDOLUS,
VARIUS.

*A brazen heart,
multifaceted in its
evil subtleties.*
Sallust
Bellum Catilinae

HOMO
AVARISSIME ET
SPURCISSIME.

*Most grasping and
most grimy of
men!*
Cicero
In Verrem II

INQUE LUTO
FIXUM POSSIS
TRANSCENDERE
NUMMUM
NEC GLUTTU
SORBERE
SALIVAM
MERCURIALEMP

*Can't you even walk
past a coin stuck
in the mud
without the venal
saliva dribbling
from your mouth?*
Persius
Satire V

VENAL

Are you really surprised, when you love money more th
Hor

GURGES AC
VORAGO
PATRIMONII.

*In you, your
inheritance
has found a
gaping abyss
leading to a
bottomless pit.*
Cicero
Pro Sestio

LIVIDE

Green-eyed monster!
Martial
Epigrams XI.20

• 51 •

DENTES
VEL SILICEM
COMESSE
POSSUNT.

*Those teeth of
yours could
chew up a a
flint-stone.*
Catullus
poem 23

LUPATRIA

Wolf-eyed woman!
Petronius
Satyricon

TURBIDA
RAPACIOR
PROCELLA.

*You are more voracious
than a ravening
whirlwind.*
Catullus
poem 25

LECHEROUS

NON TAM
LATERA ECFUTUTA PANDAS,
NI TU QUID FACIAS INEPTIARUM.
You wouldn't look this clapped-out,
if you hadn't been up to
no good!
Catullus, poem 6

EGO IRACUNDUS SUM, ET
TU LIBIDINOSUS: VIDE, QUAM
NON CONVENIAT HIS MORIBUS.
I am a grumpy old sod, and you are
obsessed with sex; you see —
we are not really compatible.
Petronius, Satyricon

TANDEM
IMPETRAVI UT
EGOMET ME CORRUMPEREM
At last! I've finally managed to
completely screw up my life!
Plautus, Mercator

LIBIDINOSUS

NAM QUOD IN AETATEM INCREPUISTI, TANTUM ME ABESSE PUTO AB IMPUDICITIA, QUANTUM TU A PUDICITIA.

As for all the insinuations you have made against my life, I believe that I am as far from Vice as you are from Virtue.

Pseudo-Cicero, In Sallustium

PATHICE

Catamite!

Catullus poem 16

CINAEDE

Sodomite!

Catullus poem 16

PRAETEREA SANCTUM NIHIL EST
NEQUE AB INGUINE TUTUM,
NON MATRONA LARIS, NON FILIA VIRGO, NEQUE IPSE
SPONSUS LEVIS ADHUC, NON FILIUS ANTE PUDICUS;
HORUM SI NIHIL EST, AVIAM RESUPINAT AMICI.

Nothing is sacred, nothing is safe from his private parts;
not the lady of the house, nor the virgin daughter,
not even the cute son-in-law to-be,
and not the innocent son and heir;
if none of these is available,
he will fling his friend's grandmother on her back.
Juvenal, Satire 3

CONTRA MARITORUM
INEFFICACES DILIGENTIAS
CONSTANTISSIMUS!

All the futile precautions of husbands
come to nothing when set against the
doggedness of his determination.
Apuleius, Metamorphoses IX

IAM VERO QUAE TANTA
UMQUAM IN ULLO
IUVENTUTIS INLECEBRA FUIT
QUANTA IN ILLO? QUI ALIOS
IPSE AMABAT TURPISSIME,
ALIORUM AMORI
FLAGITIOSISSIME SERVIEBAT.

Now who ever managed to lure in as
much young flesh as he did, fulfilling his
own filthy longings with some of them,
and pandering to the
degenerate desires of others?
Cicero, In Catilinam II

NIMIAST MISERIA NIMIS PULCHRUM
ESSE HOMINEM.
How unbearably tiresome it is to be too handsome!
Plautus, Miles Gloriosus

POPULI ODIUM QUIDNI NOVERIM, MAGNIDICUM,
CINCINNATUM MOECHUM UNGUENTATUM.
*How could I possibly have avoided making the acquaintance of
this public nuisance, this big-mouthed, curly-headed, perfume-
soused womaniser?*
Plautus, Miles Gloriosus

AEGRAE SOLAQUE LIBIDINE
FORTES DELICIAE...
*A debilitated dandy in fine fettle only
for fornication...*
Juvenal, Satire 4

...ARDENS IN CUPIDITATIBUS
...Writhing in the flames of his lust.
Sallust, Bellum Catilinae

VOCES FALLACIS AMICAE
Perfidious pillow-talk.
Ovid
Amores II.9

O MISERAE MULIERIS
FECUNDITATEM CALAMITOSAM
Such a shabby specimen of femininity, overflowing
with the spawn of the devil!
Cicero, Philippicae II

...MULIER NIGRIS DIGNISSIMA BARRIS.
...The kind of woman who could only be satisfied
by a big black elephant.
Horace, Epode 12

PUELLA DEFUTUTA...
A thoroughly tried and tested nymphomaniac...
Catullus, poem 41

.PSALLERE ET SALTARE
ELEGANTIUS, QUAM NECESSE EST PROBAE.
...Plucking the lyre and gyrating her hips with a lot
more dexterity than is needed by a decent woman.
Sallust, Bellum Catilinae

PRIMA HOMINIS FACIES ET PULCHRO PECTORE VIRGO
PUBE TENUS, POSTREMA IMMANI CORPORE PISTRIX,
DELPHINUM CAUDAS UTERO COMMISSA LUPORUM.
She has a human face and the body of a lovely young girl, until below the
*waist; but under **that** she's a sea-serpent of monstrous proportions, with a*
dolphin's tail joined to a wolfish womb.
Virgil, Aeneid III

SED EI CARIORA SEMPER OMNIA QUAM DECUS ATQUE PUDICITIA FUIT;
PECUNIAE AN FAMAE MINUS PARCERET, HAUD FACILE DISCERNERES.

Modesty and decency were the last things on her shopping list; and it would be difficult to work out whether she economised more stringently on her money or her reputation.

Sallust, Bellum Catilinae

SUO PUDORE POSTPOSITO TORIQUE GENIALIS CALCATO FOEDERE LAREM MARITI
LUPANARI MACULASSET INFAMIA, IAMQUE PERDITA NUPTAE DIGNITATE
PROSTITUTAE SIBI NOMEN ASCIVERIT.

She tossed her chastity out the window, trampled underfoot the bonds of holy matrimony, stained her husband's home with the reputation of a whorehouse, and having spurned the dignity of a married woman, took on the name of Prostitute.

Apuleius, Metamorphoses IX

QUAE NUBIT TOTIENS, NON NUBIT: ADULTERA LEGE EST.

*A woman who gets married **that** often doesn't get married: She just does the paperwork for her adultery.*

Martial, Epigrams VI.7

SUBANDO TENTA CUBILIA TECTAQUE RUMPIT.

In a fit of lust she bursts the bedraggled bed and raises the roof of the house. Horace, Epode 12

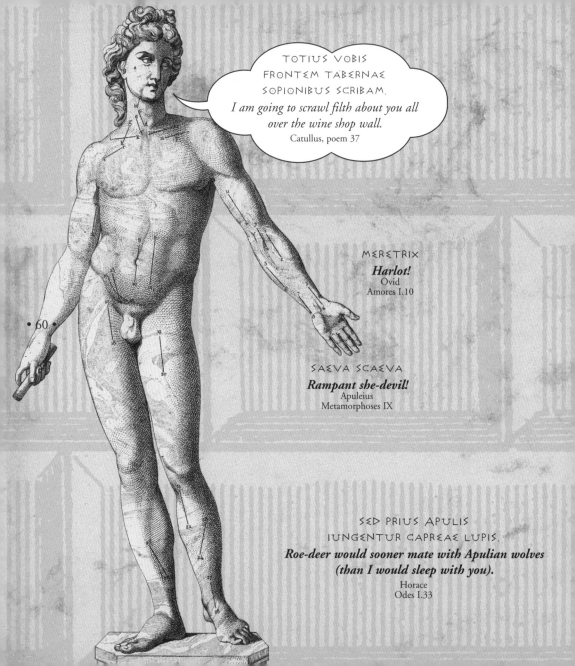

UNUS HIBERINAE VIR SUFFICIT? OCIUS ILLUD
EXTORQUEBIS, UT HAEC OCULO CONTENTA SIT UNO.

Could one man be enough for Hiberina?
She'd sooner have you poke out one of her eyes,
and be quite content with the remaining one.

Juvenal
Satire 6

HANC IN PISCINA DICOR
FUTUISSE MARINA.
NESCIO; PISCINAM ME
FUTUISSE PUTO.

Apparently we made love in
the salt-water fish-pond.
I'm not so sure.
It felt like I was making love
with the fish-pond.

Martial
Epigrams XI.21

LESBIA SE IURAT GRATIS NUMQUAM ESSE
FUTUTAM.
VERUM EST. CUM FUTUI VULT,
NUMERARE SOLET.

Lesbia swears she only does it for money,
and it's true. When she wants it,
she usually pays cash.

Martial
Epigrams XI.62

DELICIAS ILLEPIDAE

Unsavoury sweetheart.

Catullus
poem 6

HIC ERIT IN LECTO FORTISSIMUS.

He is Hercules in the sack.

Juvenal
Satire 6

MERETRIX AUGUSTA

An Empress amongst harlots.

Juvenal
Satire 6

PRODITORES

Traitors!

Cicero, In Pisonem

NUTRICULA SEDITIOSORUM OMNIUM

Wet-nurse of all traitors!

Cicero, In Vatinium

ASTUTAM VAPIDO SERVAS IN PECTORE VOLPEM.

You nurse a crafty fox in that puny breast of yours.

Persius, Satire V

NUNC MENTIS VITIO LAESA FIGURA TUA EST.

Your outward charms are mutilated by your evil mind.

Ovid, Amores I.10

SIMULATOR AC DISSIMULATOR

Dealer and double-dealer!

Sallust, Bellum Catilinae

TESTAMENTORUM SUBIECTOR

Forger of last wills and testaments!

Cicero, In Catilinam II

BELUA MULTORUM ES CAPITUM.

You are a many-headed monster.

Horace, Epistles I

CIRCUMSCRIPTOR

Bamboozler!

Cicero, In Catilinam II

MALA LINGUA

Forked tongue!

Ovid, Amores II.2

TREACHEROUS

IN MELLE
SUNT LINGUAE
SITAE VOSTRAE,
ATQUE ORATIONES
LACTEQUE: CORDA FELLE
SUNT SITA ATQUE
ACERBO ACETO.

*Your words and phrases overflow
with milk and honey;
your heart is steeped in vinegar
and bitter gall.*

Plautus
Truculentus

DOMI HABET ANIMUM
FALSILOQUOM, FALSIFICUM, FALSIIURIUM,
DOMI DOLOS, DOMI DELENIFICA FACTA,
DOMI FALLACIAS.

*Her home is piled high with an endless supply of perfidious
words, two-faced tricks and false-hearted oaths.
Piled high with ploys, piled high with provocative
seduction, piled high with lies.*

Plautus, Miles Gloriosus

NIMIS FACETE
NIMISQUE FACUNDE MALAST.

*She's as elegantly and eloquently evil
as they come!*

Plautus, Miles Gloriosus

CUSTOS DOMINUSQUE VIPERARUM

The keeper and master of the reptile-house.

Martial, Epigrams I.41

PERFIDUS

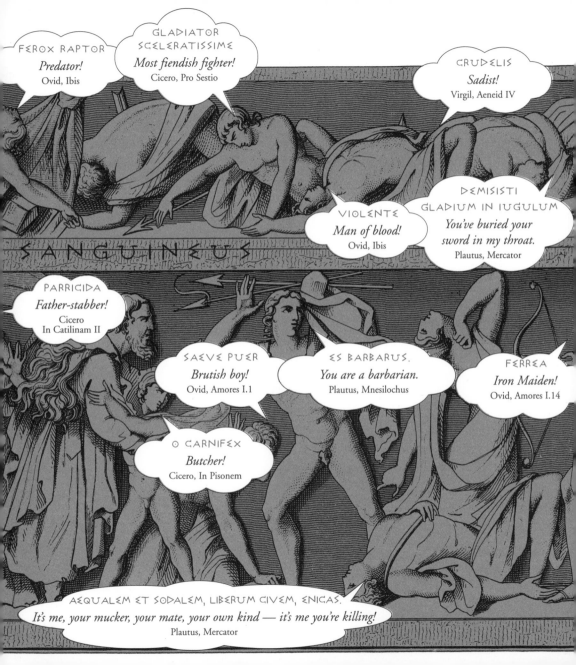

SI, COMINI, POPULI ARBITRIO TUA CANA SENECTUS
SPURCATA IMPURIS MORIBUS INTEREAT,
NON EQUIDEM DUBITO QUIN PRIMUM INIMICA BONORUM
LINGUA EXECTA AVIDO SIT DATA VULTURIO,
EFFOSSOS OCULOS VORET ATRO GUTTURE CORVUS,
INTESTINA CANES, CETERA MEMBRA LUPI.

If, Cominius, your decrepit old age, polluted by your wicked ways, should be cut short by the will
of the people, I have no doubt that it will be your tongue, the enemy of all good men, which
will be cut out first, and thrown to the greedy vulture; the raven will suck your
gouged-out eyes down its dark black throat, the dogs will guzzle your
guts. And the leftovers? The wolves will get them!

Catullus, poem 108

• 66 •

rhinocerotis *turpiculo puella naso*
SOLITATOR cincinnatus *vastus animus* RIDICULI peronatus arator
lacticulosus stulte LIPPE *schoenobates* larva
CAEPA CIRRATA *odiosus mihis* larva
arifuga *vervex* LIGNEA verbero LONGINQUUS PISCIS
SATELLITES *senex hircosus* livide *sex hara producta* arifuga ve
insapiens ILLEPIDAE DELICIAE SALIVA MUCUSQUE SATELL
nasum rhinocerotis *caenum* *turpiculo puella naso* *insapiens*
ursis asperior pilosior que lichenes
MALA PITUITA NASI *febriculosi* CAENUM MALA PIT
senex nequissime *larva* sceleratus *odiosus mihis* senex nequ
SOLITATOR *vastus animus* RIDICULI peronatus arator SOLITATOR
cincinnatus stulte LIPPE *schoenobates* molestae *lacticulosus* cincinna
lacticulosus CAEPA CIRRATA *odiosus mihis* CAE
arifuga *vervex* verbero arifuga *ver*
SATELLITES *senex hircosus* livide producta arifuga *ver*
insapiens ILLEPIDAE DELICIAE *naso* *insapiens*
nasum rhinocerotis *caenum* *turpiculo puella naso* gum rhin
MALA PITUITA NASI *febriculosi* lichenes MALA PIT
nex nequissime *larva* sceleratus *mihis* senex neq
cincinnatus *schoenobates* cincinna
lacticulosus stulte LIPPE *schoenobates* *lacticulosus*
arifuga *vervex* verbero
SATELLITES *senex hircosus* *hara producta* arifuga *ver*
sapiens ILLEPIDAE puella naso *insapiens*
sum rhinocerotis ursis asperior nequissime lichenes livide rhino
MALA PITUITA NASI *febriculosi* CAENUM
ex nequissime *larva* sceleratus *odiosus mihis* senex nequiss
SOLITATOR RIDICULI peronatus arator SOLITATOR
cincinnatus *schoenobates* cincinnatus
lacticulosus *odiosus mihis* larva molestae *lacticulosus*
uga *vervex* verbero arifuga *vervex*
SATELLITES *senex hircosus* livide producta arifuga *vervex*
MALA PITUITA *caenum* *turpiculo puella naso* *insapiens*